Overdrive
Life, Led by The Holy Spirit

Steve Kelly

Introduction

As of this writing, there are over one billion cars on planet Earth.[1] In the past one hundred years, cars have advanced from novelty machine to a primary source of daily transportation for human beings, products, and food.

Motor vehicles have benefited from many improvements in design and performance during the past century. From rubber tires to ignition switches to air bags, cars have evolved over the years to become lighter, safer and faster.

The introduction of Overdrive in the middle of the 20th century was a significant improvement that gave cars and trucks much longer life and fuel efficiency.

An Overdrive is a mechanism that allows an automobile to cruise at high speeds with reduced engine RPM. This leads to better fuel economy, lower noise, and less wear and tear.[2]

In modern cars, the Overdrive is an additional gearbox that is built into the transmission and enables the engine to run fast without strain and burnout.

Because of Overdrive, cars and trucks can run at high speeds for long distances without overheating.

1   http://www.huffingtonpost.ca/2011/08/23/car-population_n_934291.
html
2   http://en.wikipedia.org/wiki/Overdrive_(mechanics)

They can be driven for thousands upon thousands of miles without damaging or breaking vital engine parts.

If you've read this far, you're probably thinking, "Ok, I'm glad cars run better, but what does that have to do with the Holy Spirit?" You're about to find out.

You see, just like a car engine benefits from having a built-in Overdrive, the Christian benefits in remarkable ways from having the indwelling presence of the Holy Spirit.

A car can function without Overdrive. It will, however, have a limited range and capacity. It will strain and struggle. It will have a greater need for repair and replacement parts.

Christians can and often do function without the constant presence of the Holy Spirit. But without Him, we have a limited range and capacity. We strain and stretch but are never able to run smoothly and efficiently for extended periods at high speeds, which is what God desires. What our heart desires.

Which is why God sent Christians the ultimate drivetrain – The Holy Spirit. He put in the believer His version of Overdrive. Get ready to go farther, faster, than you ever dared imagine.

Overdrive: Life Led by the Holy Spirit.

First Gear

Unlike the Overdrive, a recent invention, the Holy Spirit has always existed. As part of the Trinity, or three parts of God, the Holy Spirit was present at Creation. The second verse of the Bible tells us "The Spirit of God hovered over the waters."[3]

The rest of the Old Testament provides many illustrations of the Holy Spirit's function and purpose. **During the Old Covenant, before Jesus came, the Holy Spirit's role was limited and momentary.**

The Old Covenant was simple: God said, "Obey my voice and I will be your God. And you will be my people."[4]

This agreement was quickly broken by the Israelites, in part because **they didn't have the indwelling power of the Holy Spirit.** They were trying to keep God's commands through their own will power.

Like cars without Overdrive, they strained with all their might to keep the pace. And like cars without Overdrive, they inevitably burned out, snapped and broke down. They couldn't run very fast for very long.

---

3   *Genesis 1:2*
4   *Jeremiah 7:23*

In the early days, the Overdrive was a bolt-on mechanism that could be added to a car's gearbox. It could be connected to the transmission to be used for a long trip or heavy load.

After the work was done, it could be removed.

Under the Old Covenant, God would send the Holy Spirit for a specific mission that required endurance and power. After that mission was over, the Holy Spirit left.

The Holy Spirit was Momentary

One man who personified the momentary experience of the Holy Spirit during the Old Testament was Samson. Samson was a judge of Israel.

Samson is probably best known for losing his power to the deceitful woman Delilah. But Samson did some amazing things, thanks to the power of the Holy Spirit.

Before Samson was born, an Angel of the Lord told his parents that Samson would "begin to deliver Israel out of the hand of the Philistines."[5]

Samson grew up and became a judge of Israel.

---

5   *Judges 13:5*

As he traveled about the country, he encountered physical attacks: first from a lion, then from Philistine men.

In each circumstance, the Spirit "came mightily upon him", and he was victorious.[6]

When the Holy Spirit came upon Samson, he was given supernatural physical strength. He was like a fictional character from a super hero comic book.

He literally tore the lion to pieces. He killed thirty men in one fight. Later, when he was tied up by the Philistines, **the Spirit once again came mightily upon him and he killed 1,000 men by himself.**[7]

Astonishing. Unbelievable. Samson was a one-man Philistine wrecking crew. But **only when the Holy Spirit came upon him.** Because it was the Old Covenant, the Holy Spirit's empowerment was temporary, just for the need of the moment.

Samson grew used to the Holy Spirit's power and began to think he was doing these incredible feats through his own strength.

Delilah was attractive. She was seductive. Samson was full of himself; he was overconfident, even arrogant. He believed he could play with fire and walk away not only

---

6   *Judges 14:6, 19*
7   *Judges 15:14-15*

un-singed but he wouldn't even smell like smoke!

She begged and cajoled him and he finally told her where his strength came from. He fell asleep and she called the Philistines to come. She woke him up shouting, "The Philistines are upon you!"[8]

He jumped up to fight them and he said, "I will break free!" But a very sad thing happened – **He did not know the Spirit had left him.**

Samson took the presence of the Holy Spirit for granted and didn't even realize, when he needed it most, the power of God was gone.

Unlike Samson's experience, no longer is the Holy Spirit's presence momentary. He is not a "bolt-on" Overdrive that comes only for special missions. **Because of the New Covenant, and through the baptism of the Holy Spirit, He is permanent.**

We don't have to pray for Him to show up and rescue us. We get to pray with Him, as He prays through us to empower us every day to overcome every situation. Because the Holy Spirit is **permanent,** we can conquer every circumstance. We can run our race at top speed without burnout or breakdown.

The Holy Spirit was External

Samson was a powerful judge, and he accomplished mighty works. But he only received temporary help from the Spirit, and when he didn't have the Spirit, he got captured. He had his eyes gouged out and was turned into a slave for his people's enemy, the Philistines. Not a good end.

After the judges, God gave Israel kings to rule over them. King David is probably the most famous of them all. He was described as a "Man after God's own heart."[9]

Yet, for as great as David was, and for all the incredible Psalms he wrote, David experienced a continual challenge to stay in God's presence because under the **Old Covenant, the Holy Spirit's work was external.**

Just like the early Overdrive was an add-on that connected to the outside of a car's transmission, **the Holy Spirit moved on men and woman from above and without, not from within.**

David was just a boy when Samuel the prophet was sent by God to anoint him as king. Samuel listened for God's voice as he viewed all of David's older brothers. God didn't say anything until he finally got to David.

---

9   *I Samuel 13:13*

As Samuel stood before the teenage shepherd, God said, "Arise, anoint him, for this is the one!"[10] As Samuel poured the anointing oil on David, the Holy Spirit came upon the young future king. **The Holy Spirit came on him; He did not come through him**.

David went on to defeat Goliath, through the power of the Holy Spirit. He became King after years of trials and hiding from the murderous King Saul.

He faced temptation and he sinned. He repented and he was restored. He was human, just like us. He fought battles and slayed nations. Sometimes, he ran for his life. Through it all, King David repeatedly pleaded with God to "not take your Spirit from me."[11]

If he was anointed, why did King David have to ask for the Spirit to remain?

Because under the Old Covenant, he had a Holy Spirit who worked only from the outside in.

Like that old Overdrive mechanism that was bolted on from the outside, and was removed from time to time, the Holy Spirit of the Old Testament was temporary and came "upon" people.

---

10   *I Samuel 16:13*
11   *Psalm 51:11*

An improvement to the Overdrive allowed it to be embedded within the transmission of cars and trucks in the 1960's. This was a great advancement and a welcome innovation.

While the Internal Overdrive is nice for cars, **what Jesus did through ushering in the New Covenant was miraculous**. It was transformative. No longer would the Holy Spirit come and go. No longer would He come upon the believer from without.

Now, the Holy Spirit is *PERMANENT.*
Now, the Holy Spirit works *FROM WITHIN.*

Second Gear

The New Covenant changed everything. Jesus's death and resurrection brought to life a new agreement between God and His people. In this New Covenant, God made the same promise He had made with the Israelites, with two significant changes.

1. **He made the New Covenant available for all people**. Not just the Israelites, but every human. "To as many as receive Jesus are given the right to become children of God."[12]

2. He would no longer require the believers to live up to His standard by their own power. He gave them – *us* – the Holy Spirit. **The Holy Spirit enables us to keep our end of the bargain.**

The Holy Spirit through us gives us the power to be the "unceasing, universal, all-sufficient worker of everything that has to be produced by the Christian."[13]

Like the Overdrive fitted internally in a vehicle's transmission, accepting Jesus as your Lord and Savior means His

---

12   John 1:12
13   Sumner, Tracy. *The Essential Works of Andrew Murray. Barbour Publishing, 2008, USA. pp. 40*

Spirit comes in and resides. He abides. We don't have to plead like King David to God "take not your Spirit from me!"

The Holy Spirit is Permanent

God will never take the Holy Spirit from us. Jesus made this promise after He told His disciples about Judas's impending betrayal and His coming crucifixion.
The disciples were with Jesus during The Last Supper, and Jesus wanted to wash his disciples' feet. Peter, the impetuous, temperamental one, told Jesus, "You will never wash my feet!"[14]

Peter thought it would be disrespectful for Jesus to do such a menial task. He knew Jesus was the Son of God and he couldn't imagine having God Almighty washing his dirty toes!

Jesus replied, "If I don't wash your feet, you will have no part with Me."
Peter instantly cried, "Then don't just wash my feet! Wash my hands and my head, too!"

After Jesus washed his disciples feet, He told them that Judas would betray Him. He told them that He would be leaving. The disciples didn't understand that He was talking about His crucifixion.

---

14   John 13:8-9

The disciples were very troubled. They couldn't imagine life without Jesus. He was young, only thirty-three years old. They wanted to be with Him for the rest of their lives!

They asked Him why He had to go. He told them He was going to prepare their place in God's Kingdom. Then He made an awesome promise. He told them that when He left, He would send the Holy Spirit, Who would *abide FOREVER.*[15]

Though the disciples didn't comprehend all that was about to happen, we understand today what Jesus was talking about.

Jesus was about to die for the sins of all people. He was about to be buried and then resurrected. And when He did all this, He was going to send the Holy Spirit.

Then, **the Holy Spirit would stay with us permanently.***[16]*

When Jesus ascended, he sent the Holy Spirit, who provides Christians with the power to drive through life without fear and condemnation.

What great comfort! We don't have to push with all our might. We don't have to run until we collapse, exhausted and broken. We get to rely on the Overdrive of the Holy

---

15   *John 14:16*
16   *1John 2:27*

Spirit, working on our behalf 24/7.

The Holy Spirit *abides* with us and teaches us all things. The permanent abiding power of the Holy Spirit guides us through life.

Because of the Holy Spirit's permanent presence, we can call on His strength every moment, to drive us forward and onward, at speeds we didn't think possible, to destinations we scarcely imagined we'd see.

The Holy Spirit is Internal

The Holy Spirit is not only permanent, but thanks to the New Covenant, He is also internal. As Jesus said to the disciples, *"He Abides."*

Thanks to Jesus, every Christian has, like the modern Overdrive, the Holy Spirit placed within them. He is no longer external, working from the outside in. **He is now internal, working from the inside out.**

The Holy Spirit in us brings great power. He brings something that is necessary for us to accomplish all that God desires. **The essential element of the Holy Spirit's work in us is the operation of God's grace.**

All the challenges, temptations and trials that we face on this earth can be overcome through His grace. Through His grace in us, we are able to experience the "abundance we need to do every good work."[17]

Put another way by the late theologian Andrew Murray, "Grace is not only the power that moves the heart of God, it is also the power that moves the heart of the Christian and provides it each moment with the power to love God and do His will."

This grace comes by way of the internal dwelling of the Holy Spirit. Like the Overdrive, it is this internal permanent placement of the Holy Spirit that gives us the grace and strength to accomplish great things. Things we could never have accomplished on our own.

He is permanent and internal. But what exactly, is He? Who is the Holy Spirit?

---

17   *2 Corinthians 9:8*

Third Gear

The Holy Spirit is described with many terms throughout the Bible. A few of them are listed here:

Helper – "The Holy Spirit…will teach you all things and bring to your remembrance all things that I said to you." (John 14:26)

Comforter – "Then the churches…had peace. And walking in the fear of the Lord and in the comfort of the Holy Spirit, they were multiplied." (Acts 9:31)

Advocate – "And when He (the Holy Spirit) has come, He will convict the world of sin and of righteousness and of judgment." (John 16:8)

Guide – "He will guide you into all truth; for He will not speak on His own authority, but whatever He hears He will speak; and He will tell you things to come." (John 16:13)

The Holy Spirit is our permanent, internal voice of God. He speaks hope when we are in despair. He speaks truth when we are deceived. He shows us the next step when our path is dark. He gives us the extra gear we need when we have no more rev in our engine.

He is accessible constantly. He is always waiting to help us. He even prays to God for the will of God to be done on our behalf.[18]

Those who aren't Christians are not able to access the Holy Spirit. They are like cars before Overdrive. They grind their gears and redline their engine, hoping to accomplish their dreams. In the end, they are frustrated and resentful because they simply don't have the extra gear necessary to smoothly and consistently drive through life.

We do. The believer can, because of the Holy Spirit.

The Holy Spirit is our guide, our comforter, and our intercessor. He works through us and in us to teach us and lead us.

Jesus promised that the Holy Spirit would give us power. In fact, His very last recorded statement to the disciples as He ascended to heaven was exactly that.

He said, "You shall receive power when the Holy Spirit has come upon you."[19]

Jesus wouldn't lie. He can't lie. The Holy Spirit is our permanent, internal overdrive. Why then do we often still feel depleted? Why is our energy sapped and why does it feel like our parts are wearing thin?

---

18   *Romans 8:27*
19   *Acts 1:8*

There is more to the Holy Spirit than just reading about Him in the Scripture. There must be a way that we can be certain of His grace. There must be evidence of His work on our behalf.

There is! Shortly after Jesus told his disciples that they would receive power, they gathered together to pray. They waited, as Jesus instructed.

He told them to remain in Jerusalem until they received the power of the Holy Spirit.[20]

The Holy Spirit brings Power

As they remained waiting, suddenly the room was filled with the sound of a "rushing mighty wind."[21] It filled the entire room. Then they saw fire, like a divided tongue, above everyone's head. As if that wasn't unusual enough, they all began to speak with "other tongues" as they were filled with the Holy Spirit.

This event is known as the Day of Pentecost. In that moment, God's Overdrive was installed permanently and internally. Everyone in that room was filled with the Holy Spirit and was empowered to build the Church. To bring the Kingdom of Heaven to Earth.

---

20   *Luke 24:49*
21   *Acts 2:2-4*

Peter preached his first sermon that day. The power of the operation of the Holy Spirit through him and the other disciples led to 3,000 people accepting Christ.

In One Day.

The Holy Spirit enabled the disciples to spread the gospel throughout the world. He enabled them to raise the dead, to cast out demons, to heal the sick. The Holy Spirit's power took over their lives and drove them to great success for the purposes and glory of God.

They were so powerful and unstoppable that when the Jewish leaders who didn't believe in Jesus described them, they said, "They have turned the world upside down…"[22]

Wow! That's power! **How can we live in such a way that we would be described as "turning the world upside down"?**

Though the Holy Spirit comes into your life when you accept Jesus as your Savior, there is another manifestation of His power and presence in your life.

This manifestation is the same outward demonstration that happened when the disciples received the Holy Spirit, speaking in other tongues - also known as a heavenly prayer language.

---

22   *Acts 17:6*

A few years after Pentecost, the Apostle Paul was in Ephesus, a city in the country we now call Turkey. He visited some of the new converts and asked them if they had received the Holy Spirit.

They told him, "We had not heard there was a Holy Spirit."[23]

Paul laid hands on them and the Holy Spirit came upon them. And the same thing that happened on the Day of Pentecost happened to those men that day. **They spoke in other tongues.**

How can you receive the ultimate that God has for you? How can you live in Overdrive every day, all day long? By receiving the Baptism of the Holy Spirit and your heavenly prayer language.

This language is the language of God, uttered through you by the Holy Spirit. In so doing, **the Holy Spirit prays for you the perfect will of God for you**.

Once you receive the baptism of the Holy Spirit and pray in the Spirit regularly, you'll discover a whole new source of power. A whole new source of energy. A whole new gear. **Overdrive.**

---

23   *Acts 19:1-2*

Fourth Gear

The Baptism of the Holy Spirit has been a source of confusion and controversy throughout the history of the Church. It enables the believer to communicate with God without interference from the flesh, the devil or the natural mind.

It's designed to equip you to pray exactly how God would have you pray. **It's the Holy Spirit's way of helping you talk directly to God the Father**.

No wonder there's been confusion over the topic - if Satan can get Christians to avoid praying in the Spirit, he could short-circuit the Overdrive system God has installed. He could prevent Christians from going the distance. From having all the power they need, whenever they need it.

This book is not intended to clarify the gift of tongues. It is designed to lead people to an understanding of the need for and to receive the Baptism of the Holy Spirit.

Evidence of Baptism of the Spirit

As already mentioned, the Baptism of the Spirit gives the Christian an added dimension of power and communication with Heaven.

When Jesus was with the disciples, this prayer language was unnecessary. They could talk to Him because He was with them in the flesh.

When He left Earth, He knew they would need all the power of Heaven to help them not only survive the persecution they were about to face, but also to thrive and build the hope of the world, the local church.

The Baptism of the Spirit was His plan. Prayer in the Spirit is God's strategy to keep the forces of darkness and man's weak flesh from interfering with His download of grace and courage to the Christian.

The Baptism of the Spirit releases the prayer language of the believer. The evidence of the Baptism of the Spirit is the ability of the believer to pray in a new tongue, or language.[24] **The purpose of the heavenly prayer language is to edify, or encourage and strengthen, the Christian.[25]**

Typically, a Christian receives this Baptism through prayer with fellow believers or pastors. The Apostle Paul modeled the way when he met with the men in Acts 19 who had never heard about the Baptism of the Spirit. **He laid hands on them, the Holy Spirit came upon them, and they spoke with tongues.**

---

24   *Acts 19:6*
25   *I Corinthians 14:4*

At first, it may feel strange and uncomfortable. But that's usually because we are focused on what people may think about us saying words that we don't understand. But God understands. And that's the point. Once we recognize the power of the Baptism of the Holy Spirit, and the truth of its reality and relevance for every day life, we find great strength from it.

The apostle Paul, who wrote most of the books of the New Testament, had this to say about praying in the Spirit: *"I thank God that I pray in the Spirit more than you all."* [26]

Paul recognized its importance and declared that he prayed in the Spirit all the time. **One great thing about the Baptism of the Holy Spirit is that you can "pray without ceasing."** [27]

Throughout your day, under your breath, or at the top of your lungs (when you're by yourself – more on the need for order in a minute), you can pray in the Spirit. You can edify yourself to go further and be greater, thanks to the Baptism of the Holy Spirit, thanks to your heavenly prayer language.

---

26   *I Corinthians 14:18*
27   *I Thessalonians 5:17*

7 STEPS TO LEADING SOMEONE IN THE BAPTISM OF THE HOLY SPIRIT:

1. Explain the need (Acts 1:8, John 7:37)
2. Explain the difference between being born of and being filled with the Spirit (John 7:37-39)
3. Explain that the promise of the Spirit is for all Christians. (Acts 2:39, Galatians 3:14)
4. Explain the consistent initial evidence of the Holy Spirit's "filling". (Acts 2:4; 10:44-46; 19:2-6)
5. Pray for them and lay hands on them. (Acts 9:12, 17; 8:17; 19:6)
6. Encourage them by explaining the Holy Spirit's presence and God's desire to give the Holy Spirit. (Luke 11:13)
7. Believe they will receive and pray accordingly. (Acts 19:6)

Praying in the Spirit

Some of the confusion surrounding the doctrine of the Baptism in the Spirit stems from just that – **confusion**. Often, churches have allowed people to engage in loud, disorderly praying in the Spirit. This practice confuses non-believers (and frankly, many believers as well).

The Apostle Paul once again provides pertinent instruction on the timing and use of Praying in the Spirit. After he told the church at Corinth that he "prayed in the Spirit more than all of you", He then added, "**In church, I would rather speak five words that people can understand, so I may teach people, rather than in a tongue (prayer language).**[28]

He further explains, "if the whole church is meeting and everyone starts praying in tongues, and there are unbelievers in the congregation, won't they say that you are out of your mind?"[29]

The key is that **praying in the Spirit is for *personal edification*.** The gifts of the Spirit, which are outlined in the next chapter, are for *corporate edification.*

There is an important distinction to be made here, which is tongues is a *sign* of the Baptism of the Holy Spirit, but it is also a *spiritual gift.*

Tongues as a Sign

The sign of tongues is a consistently demonstrated consequence of the Baptism of the Holy Spirit. It happened repeatedly in the New Testament. When Jesus appeared on Earth after His resurrection, He told the disciples, "… these *signs* will follow those who believe…they will speak with new tongues."[30]

---

28   *I Corinthians 14:18*
29   *I Corinthians 14:23*
30   *Mark 16:17*

This *sign* is evidence to everyone of the filling of the Holy Spirit. A key distinction between the *sign* of tongues and the *gift* of tongues is the need for interpretation.

The gift of tongues, which will be covered in the next section of this book, requires an interpretation. The sign of tongues, as shown multiple times in the book of Acts, requires no interpretation. In the day of Pentecost (Acts 2:4), they spoke in tongues, and no one interpreted.

Later, Peter is preaching to the Gentiles and many of the Jewish believers were astonished. Why? Because, "the gift of the Holy Spirit had been poured out on the Gentiles also. **For they heard them speak with tongues** and magnify God."[31]

The sign of tongues follows those who believe and is evidence of the Baptism of the Holy Spirit. It can be done in a personal and a group setting, and it does not require interpretation. It is simply a demonstration of the infilling of the Holy Spirit.

God intended to give you a powerful connection to Him. Jesus said He would not leave us as orphans.[32] He sent the Holy Spirit, and the Baptism of the Holy Spirit, to give us strength to move forward.

---

31   *Acts 12:45-46*
32   *John 14:18*

Praying in the Spirit is personal evidence of the Baptism of the Spirit, and is the higher gear for a Christian to be energized to move through life in Overdrive.

Overdrive

This final section explains the operation of the gifts of the Holy Spirit. The gifts of the Spirit are for use within the church, and in the outside world. These gifts can be exercised individually and corporately. In the previous chapter, the use and sign of tongues is described as being primarily for the individual. **The gifts of the Spirit are for the benefit of the collective, the Body of Christ, the local church.**

We understand the history of the Holy Spirit, and the history of the Overdrive. The permanent, internal overdrive mechanism enables cars and trucks to drive further, faster with less wear and tear.

The Holy Spirit enables the Christian to live a life that is "exceedingly, abundantly beyond anything we can ask or imagine, **according to the power that works in us.**"[33]

The power that works in us is the Holy Spirit. Receiving the Baptism of the Spirit gives us our heavenly prayer language, which edifies us and communicates to Heaven when we are at a loss for words. Or even when we're not.

As if that weren't already enough, God also has given the Christian specific abilities, or gifts, found in the power

---

33   *Ephesians 3:20*

of the Holy Spirit. These gifts are explained in full in 1 Corinthians chapters 12-14.

Paul explains that these gifts are available to all Christians. The Holy Spirit works them all through various believers, at various times, as He wills.[34]

We learn from Paul that these gifts are like parts of the human body – each one has a specific purpose – when each one is in operation, the entire body is healthier and stronger.

Finally, Paul teaches that anyone can operate in the gifts of the Spirit. He encourages us to "earnestly desire the greater gifts."[35]

The gifts of the Spirit are varied and many. When the gifts of the Spirit are in operation, the local church can hum along more smoothly, and accomplish great feats over great distances.

Word of Wisdom

A word of wisdom is a supernatural thought that comes directly from the Holy Spirit. It can be an answer to a question, an idea for a business, or the right response to a family crisis.

---

34   I Corinthians 12:11
35   I Corinthians 12:31

An Old Testament example was when King Solomon, the wisest man who ever lived, was faced with a very strange dilemma. Two women, who were roommates, came to his court.

They shared a bed, and they both had infant children. During the night, one of the babies had died. When they approached King Solomon, both women claimed the baby was hers.

There was no DNA sampling available in 800 B.C. There was no fingerprint analysis lab in the back of the King's palace. How could he resolve this issue?

He prayed for wisdom, and the Holy Spirit gave him an answer. He turned to the women and announced, "Well, since we don't know whose baby this is, we will just cut him in half and give each of you half."[36]

That may seem preposterous, but it worked. It was the wisdom of God. The woman whose baby was dead agreed with King Solomon. The other woman, whose baby was alive, cried out, "NO! Give the baby to her!" She would rather have another woman raise her child than allow him to be killed.

That word of wisdom gave Solomon the answer and he gave the baby to his mother. Pray for the Holy Spirit to

---

36   I Kings 3:16-28

give you similar wisdom during challenging circumstances. He will.

The word of wisdom is supernatural. It is not a strategy or a plan. It is a direct insertion of God's wisdom into the mind of the believer.

In the New Testament, the demonstration of this gift occurred when the Holy Spirit instructed the leaders of the church at Antioch to "separate Barnabas and Saul for the work to which I have called them."[37]

In this case, the apostolic leaders didn't have a growth development plan or a missionary expansion program. They simply heard from the Holy Spirit. They received a word of wisdom and acted upon it in obedience.

Word of Knowledge

The expression "word of knowledge" does not necessarily imply a spoken communication. It is simply an inward revelation of God's knowledge. It is information impressed upon the consciousness of a person that, without inquiry or reasoning, the person simply knows is true.

Unlike the word of wisdom, a word of knowledge is a revealing of some fact that allows the believer to know how to make a decision.

---

37   *Acts 13:2*

Jesus demonstrated this gift of the Spirit when he met the Samaritan woman at the well. In John 4, the story is told of this remarkable encounter.

She came to the well during the heat of the day because she was an outcast. She had a very bad reputation. Jesus saw her and asked her for a drink of water.

She agreed and they began to have a conversation. During the conversation, Jesus told her that He knew she had been married five times and that she was living with a man who wasn't her husband.

This Word of Knowledge, revealed by the Spirit, allowed Jesus to speak to her heart.

She ran to all her friends and declared, "Come see a man who told me all things I ever did. **Could this be the Christ**?"[38]

The Word of Knowledge in that circumstance gave Jesus a way to connect with her and reveal God's power. In your life, a word of knowledge could be brought to mind to enable you to connect with others, or to guide you into a right decision.

---

38   *John 4:29*

Prophecy

Prophecy is not preaching. It is not "anointed conversation." It is sudden inspiration. It is a message given by revelation of the Holy Spirit. It is not premeditated. It is not a function of the human mind. **It is not to expose sin to the congregation.**

That's what it's not. What is it?

Prophecy is a message given by revelation from God, spoken under Divine anointing. It is an activity of the human spirit, under the moving of the Holy Spirit, and not a function of the human mind. It is not premeditated, and it is not prepared.

It is speaking for another. In this case, it's speaking for the Holy Spirit. It is solely for encouragement. It can be predictive of the future, but it isn't always.

Rather than foretelling, a better definition of Prophecy is "forth-telling." It is God's way of telling a person how to go forth, how to proceed. We are to test the prophecy – if our spirit agrees with it, it may be useful for our lives.

Like all the gifts of the Spirit, Prophecy should occur in an orderly fashion. Paul teaches us that "two, or at the most three, prophecies should happen in a church service."[39]

---

39   *I Corinthians 14:29*

The gift of prophecy is not infallible. The prophetic words should be judged.

Some key ways to determine if a prophecy is from the Lord is as follows:

- True prophecy should encourage the people of God. (1 Corinthians 14:3)

- True prophecy should glorify Jesus Christ. (John 16:13)

- True prophecy produces liberty. (2 Corinthians 3:6)

- True prophecy agrees with the letter and the spirit of the Bible. (2 Timothy 3:16)

- True prophecy produces fruit in character and conduct that agrees with the fruit of the Holy Spirit. (Galatians 5:22-23)

The prophecy is subject to the control of the prophet.[40] If someone says they couldn't help it, that they had to speak, they are operating outside the Word of God.

All true prophecy agrees with the spirit and the letter of God's Word.

---

40   *I Corinthians 14:32*

Paul encourages all Christians to desire the gift of prophecy. When it is manifested correctly, it is a tremendous encouragement to the church.[41]

Faith

The gift of Faith is a manifestation gift for a momentary supernatural need. It is a supernatural ability to believe God's Word in spite of adverse circumstances.

The gift of Faith was demonstrated often in the New Testament, particularly in conjunction with Jesus's healing ministry. When He healed a centurion's servant, He acknowledged the Faith of the centurion (a Roman Army Officer in command of 100 soldiers).

The centurion asked Jesus to heal his servant. Jesus told him He would come to heal him, but the centurion told Jesus that He didn't need to come. The centurion knew that Jesus could heal his servant just by speaking the word.

"I've never seen such great faith, not in all of Israel!" Jesus exclaimed. The centurion was given the gift of Faith in that moment. He believed without doubt that Jesus's word would heal his servant.

---

41   *1 Corinthians 14:1, 39; 2 Timothy 1:6 .*

Healing

The gifts of healing are a supernatural impartation of the power of God to miraculously heal a physical condition or disease. The gifts of healing are not medical science. They are not "mind over matter". They are dependent entirely upon simple faith in God.

Shortly after the day of Pentecost, Peter demonstrated the power of the Spirit through healing.

He was walking into church with John when a lame man asked them for spare change. Peter said, "Silver and gold I do not have, but such as I have I give to you. In the name of Jesus, rise up and walk."[42]

The man was healed instantly. He jumped and danced and praised the Lord!

Jesus's earthly ministry was characterized by constant healing. Everywhere He went, people cried out and clamored to receive healing.

In one passage, Jesus was near Jericho and a blind man sitting by the roadside was begging. When the man heard the commotion of the crowd following Jesus, he asked the people for an explanation.

---

42   *Acts 3:6-7*

When they told him Jesus was nearby, the blind man cried out, "Jesus, Son of David, have mercy on me."[43]

The people told him to be quiet, but he yelled once again, "Jesus, Son of David, have mercy on me."

Jesus heard him and asked, "What do you want me to do for you?"

The blind man replied, "Lord, that I may receive my sight."

Jesus said, "Receive your sight, *your faith has made you well.*"

It only takes simple faith in God for the gifts of healing to manifest. In this case, the blind man received healing because he refused to be quiet. Jesus was drawn to his faith and healed his eyes.

Healing is a powerful gift of the Spirit, and praying for healing for friends and family is a powerful way to see God bless your life and the lives of others in need.

Miracles

Miracles are acts of divine power. They are events that are unexplainable by the natural mind and by our natural

---

43   *Luke 18:35-43*

experience. Miracles defy understanding. Jesus performed His first miracle at a wedding. His mother Mary came to him with a problem. The host of the wedding had run out of wine.

Jesus used the gift of Miracles to turn water into wine[44]. This was a supernatural act. Water doesn't "turn into" wine, no matter how long it sits in a jar.

You could put it in a bottle, store it in a wine cellar for 25 years, and when you retrieve it, it's still water.

Another astonishing miracle was done through Jesus when He and the disciples found themselves with a large crowd, a long distance from a city. Jesus had been preaching, and as the crowd grew, He and the disciples realized they did not have food for the people, and they were too far from a town to send them away without food.

On this occasion, Jesus took a few loaves of bread and some fish, and turned it into a meal which fed everyone in the crowd (5,000 was just the number of men in attendance. The actual crowd could have been 20,000 – 30,000 men, women and children).[45]

God uses miracles through us to show His power in unique circumstances. This amazing gift of the Spirit, like all of them, is available for Christians today.

---

44   *John 2:1-11*
45   *Matthew 14:13-21*

Discerning of Spirits

Discerning of spirits is a very important gift of the Spirit. It is used in the ministry of deliverance for people afflicted with demonic oppression or possession.

It is not the discerning of people. It is the discerning of the spirit influencing a person. It is not intended to criticize a person. It is intended to confront and defeat evil spirits.

This gift is also used to recognize false spirits in false prophets.[46] God, through John, instructs us to "test every spirit, whether they are from God, for many false prophets have gone out into the world."

The Gift of Tongues

The Gift of Tongues operates in conjunction with the Interpretation of Tongues.

The gift of tongues is not prophecy. Prophecy is God speaking to man. Tongues is man speaking to God.[47]

Although every Spirit-filled believer can speak in tongues

---

46   1 John 4:1
47   1 Corinthians 14:2

in his own personal devotions, not every Spirit-filled believer flows in the operation of the Gift of Tongues.[48]

The gift of tongues is for the purpose of public ministry. In 1 Corinthians 11-14, the Apostle Paul gives instructions on how the gift of tongues operates in church meetings. According to 1 Corinthians 14, the gift of tongues may be:

- a message from God to the congregation;
- a prayer of praise and thanksgiving from one in the congregation;
- spoken or sung.

Irrespective of whether it is spoken or sung, the gift of tongues is to be accompanied by the *interpretation of tongues* as a ministry to the congregation.

The gift of tongues is subject to certain restrictions:

- The leadership of the meeting (1 Cor. 14:40);
- The control of the one who operates in the gift (1 Cor. 14:32);
- No more than three operations in one meeting (1 Cor. 14:27);
- Must be accompanied by the Interpretation of tongues (1 Cor. 14:13, 27);

---

48   *1 Corinthians 12:30*

- If no interpreter is present, the operator of the gift must remain silent (1 Cor. 14:28);
- Each gift in tongues must be interpreted before another gift is given (1 Cor. 14:27).

The Interpretation of Tongues

The Interpretation of Tongues is speaking by the inspiration of the Holy Spirit in the known language of the assembled worshippers, *giving the meaning* of what was previously spoken through the manifestation of the gift of tongues.

The interpretation of tongues is not a natural ability. It is a *supernatural manifestation* of the Holy Spirit. The only connection between the speaker in tongues and the interpreter is the work of the Holy Spirit, who inspires both.

God has given the church these gifts, of both speaking in the gift of tongues and interpretation of tongues, so that all the people in the church can be edified, encouraged, and comforted.[49]

Any believer yielded to the Holy Spirit, chosen by the Holy Spirit, can exercise the gift of the interpretation of tongues. It is possible for the speaker in tongues to also interpret. *In fact, if no one else does interpret, then it's the*

---

49   *1 Corinthians 14:3,5*

speaker's responsibility to interpret.[50]

The interpretation of tongues should immediately follow the speaking in tongues.

God works in amazing ways, and all the gifts of the Holy Spirit are given to empower, encourage and assist the believer within his or her own life, as well as the church.

The Holy Spirit is gentle. His promptings can be so slight, we can dismiss them as momentary thoughts from our own mind. If our faith is small, our natural timidity takes over and we remain quiet.

The Holy Spirit is for every Christian. The Baptism of the Holy Spirit equips us with our prayer language. Praying in the Spirit enables us to be encouraged and to communicate with God as He desires. The Gifts of the Spirit are from God, for today, to build up the local church.

Let the Holy Spirit take the wheel of your life. Trust Him and find the strength you need to overcome every situation.

---

50   *1 Corinthians 14:13*

About the Author

Steve Kelly is the Senior Pastor of Wave Church, a Christian church with national and international influence. Wave Church's two main campuses are in Virginia Beach, Virginia. It has multi-site campuses located throughout the state of Virginia, as well as North Carolina, with more to come.

Pastor Steve's passion is to win the lost and to lead the generations to find their purpose in Christ, through the building of the local church. Wave Church's primary mission is to help people do life well and find their purpose in Christ through being planted in the local church.

22110630R00031

Made in the USA
Middletown, DE
20 July 2015